Letting Go:
" A Journey of change "

"Letting Go: A Journey of Change"

Rajendra Singh Vaghela

Published by Dr Rajendra Singh Vaghela, 2024.

"LETTING GO: A JOURNEY OF CHANGE"

First edition. November 3, 2024.

ISBN: 979-8227266491

Written by Rajendra Singh Vaghela.

DR. RAJENDRA SINGH VAGHELA

CONTENTS

Foreword

If I could give you One thing in this life I would give you The ability to see yourself from my eyes Only then You will realise How special you are To me To everyone and To to this whole universe

Introduction

Change is as constant as the phases of the moon, waxing and waning in our lives with a rhythm both beautiful and mysterious. Yet, for many of us, change remains a source of fear and uncertainty, something to be resisted rather than embraced. What if we could learn to dance with change, to flow with its currents rather than struggle against them? This is the transformative journey that "Letting Go: A Journey of Change" invites you to embark upon.

In a world that often feels chaotic and unpredictable, the need for guidance on navigating change has never been more pressing. This book offers a fresh perspective on the age-old challenge of adapting to life's ever-shifting landscape. Drawing inspiration from the celestial dance of the moon, it presents a unique framework for understanding and embracing the natural cycles of change in our own lives.

As the author of this book, I bring not only years of research and professional experience to the table but also my own personal journey of transformation. Having faced significant life changes and challenges, I've developed a deep understanding of the emotional and psychological processes involved in letting go and moving forward. This book is a distillation of those insights, combined with evidence-based strategies and practical techniques that have proven effective for countless individuals seeking to navigate change with grace and resilience.

What sets "Letting Go: A Journey of Change" apart is its holistic approach to personal transformation. Rather than offering quick fixes or surface-level solutions, this book delves deep into the core of what it means to truly embrace change. It recognizes that lasting transformation requires not just intellectual understanding, but emotional healing, mindset shifts, and practical action.

Throughout the chapters, several key themes emerge that form the backbone of this transformative journey. First and foremost is the concept of acceptance. We explore how accepting the reality of our current situation, including our past experiences and present challenges, is the critical first step in any process of change. This theme of acceptance is woven throughout the book, from acknowledging our shadows to embracing the present moment.

Another central theme is the power of mindfulness and presence. In a world that constantly pulls our attention in a thousand different directions, learning to be fully present in the here and now is a revolutionary act. We delve into practical mindfulness techniques that can help anchor us in the present, reducing anxiety about the future and regret about the past.

The book also places a strong emphasis on self-reflection and inner work. We explore techniques for diving deep into our psyche, uncovering hidden beliefs and patterns that may be holding us back from embracing change. This inner exploration is balanced with practical strategies for taking action in the outer world, recognizing that true transformation requires both internal shifts and external steps.

Resilience is another key theme that runs throughout the book. We examine what it means to be resilient in the face of change and adversity, and how we can cultivate this essential quality in our lives. From building support systems to developing a growth mindset, the book offers a comprehensive toolkit for strengthening our capacity to bounce back from life's inevitable challenges.

Finally, the book is infused with a spirit of hope and possibility. While it acknowledges the difficulties and pain that often accompany change, it also celebrates the beauty and opportunity inherent in new beginnings.

Through real-life stories and inspiring examples, readers are encouraged to see change not as something to be feared, but as a doorway to personal growth and new adventures.

While the insights and strategies in this book can benefit anyone facing change in their lives, it is particularly geared towards those who find themselves at a crossroads. Perhaps you're going through a major life transition, such as a career change, the end of a relationship, or a move to a new city. Or maybe you're simply feeling stuck, knowing that something needs to shift in your life but unsure of how to make it happen. If you've ever felt overwhelmed by change, resistant to letting go of the past, or anxious about an uncertain future, this book is for you.

"Letting Go: A Journey of Change" is also ideal for those who are interested in personal growth and self-development. If you're curious about mindfulness practices, emotional healing techniques, or strategies for building resilience, you'll find a wealth of practical information and exercises to support your journey.

By engaging with the concepts and practices outlined in this book, readers stand to gain a new perspective on change and its role in their lives. You'll develop a deeper understanding of your own patterns and reactions to change, and learn powerful techniques for navigating transitions with greater ease and grace. The mindfulness practices and self-reflection exercises will help you cultivate greater presence and self-awareness, while the strategies for letting go and embracing new beginnings will empower you to move forward with confidence and clarity.

Perhaps most importantly, readers will gain a sense of empowerment in the face of change. Rather than feeling at the mercy of external circumstances, you'll develop the tools and mindset to actively shape your response to life's transitions. You'll learn how to tap into your inner resilience, how to find opportunity in challenge, and how to use change as a catalyst for personal growth and transformation.

The journey of change is not always easy, but it is always worthwhile. As you turn the pages of this book, you'll be embarking on a transformative adventure – one that mirrors the ever-changing phases of the moon. Just as the moon waxes and wanes, shedding light even in the darkest of nights, so too will you learn to navigate the ebbs and flows of your own life with grace and wisdom.

In the chapters that follow, we'll explore the moon's phases as a powerful metaphor for change, using this celestial cycle to illuminate our own journeys of transformation. We'll begin by acknowledging our shadows – those parts of ourselves and our past that we often try to hide or ignore. Like the dark side of the moon, these shadows hold important lessons and insights, if only we have the courage to explore them.

From there, we'll delve into the art of letting go, learning how to release what no longer serves us. This can be one of the most challenging aspects of change, but it's also one of the most liberating. We'll explore practical strategies for letting go of negative thoughts, emotions, and attachments, creating space for new growth and possibilities.

As we progress through the book, we'll learn how to embrace the present moment, finding peace and clarity in the here and now. This is where the real magic of transformation happens – in the simple act of being fully present to our lives as they unfold. We'll explore mindfulness practices and daily routines that can help anchor us in the present, even amidst the swirl of change.

The journey of change often involves healing, and we'll dedicate time to understanding the healing process and how to nurture our inner selves. This includes exploring the stages of emotional healing, learning self-care practices that promote growth, and recognizing the importance of seeking support from others during challenging times.

A crucial milestone in our journey is developing acceptance – not as a passive resignation, but as an active embrace of reality that opens the door to true transformation. We'll explore what acceptance really means and how to cultivate it, even in difficult situations. Through real-life examples, you'll see how acceptance can be the key that unlocks positive change in your life.

As we continue our exploration, we'll delve into the power of mindset in shaping our experience of change. You'll learn about the difference between a fixed mindset and a growth mindset, and how adopting the latter can dramatically impact your ability to navigate transitions and challenges. We'll provide strategies for developing a growth mindset in your daily life, showing you how a shift in perspective can open up new possibilities and opportunities.

One of the most empowering aspects of this journey is learning to find joy in transition. Too often, we focus solely on the challenges and discomfort of change, missing the beauty and excitement that can accompany new beginnings. We'll share inspiring stories of individuals who have found unexpected joy through periods of transformation, and provide activities to help you recognize and appreciate your own growth.

As we near the end of our journey, we'll focus on building resilience – that essential quality that allows us to bounce back from adversity and thrive in the face of change. You'll learn practical techniques for cultivating resilience in your everyday life, and explore the crucial role that community and support systems play in fostering this inner strength.

Finally, we'll come full circle, returning to the metaphor of the new moon to explore the power of new beginnings. You'll learn how to set meaningful intentions for your future, how to stay committed to your personal growth beyond the pages of this book, and how to approach each new phase of your life with openness, curiosity, and courage.

As you embark on this journey through the pages of "Letting Go: A Journey of Change," prepare to be challenged, inspired, and transformed. The path of change is not always easy, but it is always rich with possibility. Like the moon in its endless cycle of renewal, you too have the capacity to continually grow, change, and shine your light into the world.

So take a deep breath, turn the page, and step into the transformative journey that awaits you. The moon and its wisdom are calling – are you ready to answer?

1

The Moon's Phases: A Metaphor for Change

The Moon's Phases: A Metaphor for Change

The moon has long been a source of fascination for humanity, its ever-changing face a constant reminder of the cyclical nature of life. As we gaze upon its silvery surface, we witness a celestial dance that has captivated poets, scientists, and dreamers alike for millennia. The moon's phases, with their predictable yet mesmerizing progression, offer us more than just a spectacular view; they provide a powerful metaphor for the changes we experience in our own lives.

Consider the new moon, a time when the moon is invisible to us from Earth. This phase represents beginnings, the potential for growth, and the quiet stirring of new ideas. In our lives, we often encounter periods of darkness or uncertainty, much like the new moon. These moments, though sometimes unsettling, are ripe with possibility. They offer us the chance to plant seeds of change, to set intentions, and to prepare for the growth that lies ahead.

As the days pass, a sliver of light appears in the sky – the waxing crescent. This phase symbolizes hope and the first signs of progress. In our personal journeys, this might manifest as a glimmer of understanding, a small step forward, or the first hint that our efforts are bearing fruit. It's a reminder that change, while often gradual, is indeed occurring.

The first quarter moon, half-illuminated in the sky, represents action and decision-making. This phase challenges us to overcome obstacles and make choices that align with our goals. In our lives, we frequently encounter crossroads where we must decide which path to take. The first quarter moon encourages us to trust our instincts and move forward with determination.

As the moon continues to wax, growing fuller and brighter, we enter the gibbous phase. This represents refinement and adjustment. In our personal growth, this phase might involve fine-tuning our approaches, learning from our experiences, and making necessary corrections to our course. It's a time of increasing clarity and understanding.

The full moon, in all its luminous glory, symbolizes culmination and revelation. It's a time when hidden things come to light, and we can see our situation with greater clarity. In our lives, full moon moments might be times of realization, achievement, or the fruition of our efforts. These are the times when we can fully appreciate how far we've come and the changes we've undergone.

As the moon begins to wane, we enter the disseminating phase. This represents sharing and reflection. In our personal journeys, this might be a time when we share our experiences and insights with others, contributing to their growth as well as our own. It's a phase of giving back and paying forward the lessons we've learned.

The last quarter moon, again half-illuminated but now waning, symbolizes release and letting go. This phase challenges us to release what no longer serves us, to clear space for new growth in the next cycle. In our lives, this might involve letting go of old habits, beliefs, or relationships that no longer align with who we're becoming.

Finally, we return to the dark moon, the last sliver before the new moon. This phase represents rest and renewal. It's a time for introspection, for gathering our strength, and for preparing for the next cycle of growth. In our lives, these moments of pause are crucial for integrating our experiences and readying ourselves for new challenges.

Understanding the moon's phases as a metaphor for change allows us to recognize and accept our own cycles of growth and transformation. Just as the moon's appearance shifts night after night, we too are constantly evolving. Sometimes our changes are dramatic and visible, like the shift from new moon to full moon. Other times, they're subtle and barely perceptible, like the gradual waxing or waning of the moon's light.

Change is an inherent part of life, as natural and inevitable as the moon's cycle. Yet, many of us resist change, clinging to the familiar even when it no longer serves us. We fear the unknown, the discomfort of growth, the possibility of failure. But imagine if the moon resisted its phases, if it clung to fullness and refused to wane, or if it shied away from its brightness and remained forever dark. The beauty of its cycle would be lost, and the rhythms of our world disrupted.

By embracing change, we open ourselves to the full spectrum of human experience. We allow ourselves to grow, to learn, to become more fully ourselves. Just as each phase of the moon has its own beauty and purpose, each stage of our personal growth offers unique gifts and opportunities.

The importance of recognizing and accepting our own phases of change cannot be overstated. When we understand that change is not only normal but necessary for our growth, we can approach it with curiosity and openness rather than fear and resistance. We can learn to trust the process, knowing that even in our darkest moments – our new moon phases – the potential for growth and renewal is present.

Moreover, recognizing our phases allows us to be gentler with ourselves. Just as we don't expect the moon to be full every night, we can learn not to expect constant productivity or happiness from ourselves. We can honor our need for rest and reflection during our waning phases, and celebrate our moments of fullness and achievement when they come.

As we journey through life, we will experience countless cycles of change. Some will be gradual, almost imperceptible, like the slow turning of seasons. Others will be sudden and dramatic, like the rapid shift of tides. By embracing the moon's phases as a metaphor for our own journey, we can navigate these changes with greater grace and understanding.

In the chapters that follow, we will explore various aspects of change and personal growth, drawing inspiration from the moon's eternal dance. We will delve into the shadows of our past, learn the art of letting go, and discover the power of living in the present moment. Just as the moon's light guides travelers through the night, may the wisdom gleaned from its phases illuminate our path of personal transformation. As we conclude this chapter and prepare to delve deeper into our journey of change, let us carry with us the image of the ever-changing moon. Let it remind us that change is not something to be feared, but a natural and beautiful part of our existence. In the next chapter, we will turn our gaze inward, exploring the shadows of our past and how they shape our present. Like the dark side of the moon, these shadows hold secrets and insights that, once illuminated, can guide us towards profound personal growth.

"Just like the moon waxes and wanes, our lives go through phases of growth and decline. Embracing change means understanding that transformation is a natural part of our journey, guiding us towards new beginnings and opportunities."

2

Understanding the Past: Acknowledging Our Shadows

Understanding the Past: Acknowledging Our Shadows

As we delve into the shadows of our past, we begin to understand the intricate tapestry of experiences that have shaped us into who we are today. The journey of change often requires us to confront these shadows, acknowledging the role they play in our present circumstances and emotional landscape. This chapter explores the importance of understanding our past, the techniques we can employ for self-reflection, and the significance of recognizing the emotions tied to our personal history.

Our past experiences, both positive and negative, leave an indelible mark on our psyche. They influence our beliefs, shape our behaviors, and color our perceptions of the world around us. psychologist Carl Jung once said, "Until you make the unconscious conscious, it will direct your life and you will call it fate." This profound statement underscores the importance of bringing our past experiences into the light of consciousness, where we can examine them objectively and understand their impact on our present lives.

The process of understanding our past begins with recognizing that we are not merely the sum of our experiences, but rather the product of how we have interpreted and internalized those experiences. Our memories, while often vivid and emotionally charged, are not always accurate representations of what truly occurred. Instead, they are colored by our perceptions, beliefs, and emotional state at the time of the event and during subsequent recollections. This understanding is crucial as we embark on the journey of self-reflection, as it allows us to approach our past with a sense of curiosity and openness rather than judgment or fear. Self-reflection is a powerful tool for uncovering the hidden influences of our past on our present. It requires a willingness to look inward, to ask ourselves difficult questions, and to sit with uncomfortable truths. One effective technique for self-reflection is journaling. By putting pen to paper (or fingers to keyboard), we create a safe space to explore our thoughts, feelings, and memories without fear of judgment or repercussion. The act of writing can help us to organize our thoughts, identify patterns in our behavior, and gain new insights into our motivations and fears.

Another valuable technique for self-reflection is meditation. By quieting the constant chatter of our minds, we create space for deeper insights to emerge. Mindfulness meditation, in particular, can help us to observe our thoughts and emotions without becoming entangled in them. This practice can reveal recurring themes or patterns in our thinking that may be rooted in past experiences. As we become more aware of these patterns, we can begin to question their validity and consider alternative perspectives.

Identifying past hurts is an essential aspect of understanding our personal history. These wounds, whether from childhood experiences, past relationships, or professional setbacks, can continue to influence our behavior and emotions long after the initial event has passed. The process of identifying these hurts requires courage and compassion for ourselves. It's important to approach this exploration with gentleness, recognizing that we are not seeking to assign blame or relive painful experiences, but rather to understand how these events have shaped us.

One effective way to identify past hurts is through the use of timeline exercises. By creating a visual representation of our life's significant events, we can begin to see patterns and connections that may not have been apparent before. This exercise can help us to identify pivotal moments or periods in our lives that have had a lasting impact on our emotional well-being and behavior patterns.

As we uncover these past hurts, it's crucial to acknowledge the emotions tied to these events. Emotions serve as signposts, pointing us towards areas of our lives that require attention and healing. Often, we may find that we have suppressed or ignored certain emotions related to past experiences, believing that by doing so, we can move on more quickly.

However, as psychologist and author Bessel van der Kolk notes in his book "The Body Keeps the Score," unprocessed emotions and trauma can manifest in physical symptoms and behavioral patterns long after the initial event.

Acknowledging these emotions doesn't mean dwelling on them or allowing them to control us. Rather, it means giving ourselves permission to feel what we feel without judgment. This process of emotional acknowledgment can be challenging, as it may bring up feelings of vulnerability or pain that we've long sought to avoid. However, it is through this acknowledgment that we begin the process of healing and integration.

One powerful technique for acknowledging and processing emotions tied to past events is the practice of "feeling through." This involves allowing ourselves to fully experience an emotion, noticing where we feel it in our body, and staying present with the sensation until it naturally subsides. This practice can help us to release emotions that we may have been carrying for years, creating space for new experiences and perspectives.

As we work to understand our past and acknowledge our shadows, it's important to remember that this process is not about assigning blame or getting stuck in a cycle of regret. Rather, it's about gaining a deeper understanding of ourselves so that we can make conscious choices about how we want to move forward. Our past experiences, even the painful ones, have contributed to our strength, resilience, and unique perspective on the world.

Understanding our past also allows us to develop greater empathy, both for ourselves and for others. As we recognize the complexities of our own journey, we become more understanding of the struggles and challenges faced by those around us. This increased empathy can lead to deeper, more meaningful relationships and a greater sense of connection to the world around us.

As we conclude this exploration of our past and its shadows, we stand at the threshold of a new understanding. With this newfound awareness, we are better equipped to begin the process of letting go of what no longer serves us. In the next chapter, we will delve into the art of releasing negative thoughts and emotions, exploring techniques for forgiveness and exercises to practice releasing our attachments to the past. This journey of understanding and release is not always easy, but it is through this process that we create space for growth, healing, and positive change in our lives.

"Our past experiences are like shadows that follow us, shaping our present reality. By delving into our past hurts through self-reflection, we illuminate these shadows, allowing us to heal and move forward with a newfound sense of awareness and understanding."

3

The Art of Letting Go: Releasing What No Longer Serves Us

The Art of Letting Go: Releasing What No Longer Serves Us

As we continue our journey through the phases of change, we find ourselves at a crucial juncture. Having explored the metaphor of the moon's phases and delved into the shadows of our past, we now stand at the threshold of liberation. The art of letting go is a fundamental skill in our personal growth and transformation. It is the key that unlocks the door to a lighter, more fulfilling existence.

Letting go is not a single act, but a process—a delicate dance between holding on and releasing. It requires courage, self-awareness, and often, a leap of faith. As the renowned spiritual teacher Eckhart Tolle once said, "Sometimes letting things go is an act of far greater power than defending or hanging on." This chapter will guide you through the intricacies of this powerful act, offering strategies to release what no longer serves you and embrace the freedom that follows.

At its core, letting go is about relinquishing control over things we cannot change. It's about accepting the impermanence of life and finding peace in the midst of constant flux. This process often begins with our thoughts and emotions, as these are the building blocks of our inner world. Negative thoughts and emotions can act like anchors, keeping us tethered to past hurts, regrets, and fears. Learning to release these mental and emotional burdens is the first step towards a lighter, more liberated existence.

One effective strategy for letting go of negative thoughts is the practice of mindful observation. This technique involves stepping back from your thoughts and observing them as if you were a neutral spectator. Instead of getting caught up in the narrative of your thoughts, you simply watch them come and go, like clouds passing through the sky. This practice helps create a sense of distance between you and your thoughts, making it easier to let go of those that don't serve you.

Renowned meditation teacher Jack Kornfield describes this process beautifully: "Let go of the battle. Breathe quietly and let it be. Let your body relax and your heart soften. Open to whatever you experience without fighting." By adopting this attitude of non-resistance, we can begin to loosen the grip of negative thought patterns and create space for more positive, empowering thoughts to take root.

Emotions, too, play a crucial role in the art of letting go. Often, we cling to negative emotions out of habit or fear, even when they cause us pain. The key to releasing these emotions lies in acknowledging and accepting them fully before letting them go. This may seem counterintuitive, but resistance only serves to strengthen the hold these emotions have on us. By fully feeling and accepting our emotions, we allow them to move through us and eventually dissipate.

A powerful technique for working with difficult emotions is the RAIN method, developed by meditation teacher Tara Brach. RAIN stands for Recognize, Allow, Investigate, and Nurture. First, we recognize the emotion we're experiencing. Then, we allow it to be present without trying to change or suppress it. Next, we investigate the emotion with curiosity and compassion, exploring its physical sensations and the thoughts associated with it. Finally, we nurture ourselves with self-compassion, offering kindness and understanding to ourselves in the face of difficult feelings.

As we practice letting go of negative thoughts and emotions, we may find ourselves confronted with deeper, more ingrained patterns of attachment. These could be attachments to past relationships, outdated beliefs about ourselves or the world, or even material possessions that no longer align with our values. Releasing these attachments can be challenging, but it's often necessary for our continued growth and evolution.

One powerful way to release attachments is through the practice of forgiveness. Forgiveness is not about condoning harmful actions or forgetting past hurts. Rather, it's a conscious decision to release the burden of anger, resentment, and pain that we carry. As the Buddha wisely said, "Holding onto anger is like drinking poison and expecting the other person to die." Forgiveness liberates us from the past and opens up space for healing and new possibilities.

Forgiveness is a deeply personal process, and it often requires time and patience. It begins with the willingness to forgive, even if we don't feel ready to do so fully. We can start by extending forgiveness to ourselves for any perceived mistakes or shortcomings. Self-forgiveness is a powerful act of self-love and an essential step in the letting go process.

To practice forgiveness, you might try a simple meditation. Close your eyes and bring to mind someone you wish to forgive. Visualize them in front of you and silently repeat phrases such as "I forgive you," "I release you," or "I wish you well." Notice any resistance that arises and gently let it go. Remember, forgiveness is a gift you give yourself, not something you do for others.

As we work on letting go of negative thoughts, emotions, and attachments, it's important to create new, positive habits and practices to fill the space that's been cleared. This might involve cultivating gratitude, practicing self-compassion, or engaging in activities that bring joy and fulfillment. The process of letting go is not just about releasing the old, but also about making room for the new.

One effective exercise for releasing attachments is the practice of decluttering. This can be done both physically and mentally. Start by going through your physical possessions and letting go of items that no longer serve a purpose or bring you joy. As you do this, pay attention to any emotions or thoughts that arise. You may find that letting go of physical items helps you release mental and emotional clutter as well.

For mental decluttering, try keeping a journal where you write down thoughts, beliefs, or habits you'd like to release. Next to each item, write down a positive affirmation or new belief you'd like to cultivate in its place. For example, if you're letting go of the belief "I'm not good enough," you might replace it with "I am worthy and deserving of love and success."

Another powerful technique for letting go is the practice of surrender. This doesn't mean giving up or resigning yourself to circumstances. Rather, it's about accepting what is and releasing the need to control outcomes. Spiritual teacher Gabrielle Bernstein describes surrender as "the art of letting go of your need to control your life." When we surrender, we open ourselves up to the flow of life and the possibilities that exist beyond our limited perspective.

To practice surrender, try this simple exercise: Whenever you find yourself struggling against a situation or feeling overwhelmed, take a deep breath and say to yourself, "I surrender this to the universe." Visualize yourself releasing the situation or problem, letting it float away like a balloon into the sky. Trust that the universe (or whatever higher power you believe in) will take care of it.

As we delve deeper into the art of letting go, it's important to acknowledge that this process can sometimes bring up feelings of fear or uncertainty. We may worry about what will fill the space left by the things we release, or fear that we're losing a part of ourselves. It's crucial to approach this process with gentleness and self-compassion, recognizing that these fears are normal and part of the journey.

Remember, letting go is not about erasing the past or denying our experiences. It's about freeing ourselves from the weight of what no longer serves us so that we can move forward with lightness and clarity. As author Melody Beattie beautifully puts it, "Letting go doesn't mean we don't care. Letting go doesn't mean we shut down. Letting go means we stop trying to force outcomes and make people behave. It means we give up resistance to the way things are, for the moment. It means we stop trying to do the impossible—controlling that which we cannot—and instead, focus on what is possible—which usually means taking care of ourselves."

As we practice the art of letting go, we may find that it becomes easier over time. Like any skill, it improves with practice. We begin to recognize more quickly when we're holding onto something that no longer serves us, and we become more adept at releasing it. This doesn't mean we'll never struggle or face challenges, but we'll have developed the tools and resilience to navigate them more skillfully.

The journey of letting go is ongoing, a continuous process of release and renewal. As we move forward, we'll find that each act of letting go creates space for something new to enter our lives—new experiences, new relationships, new perspectives. It's a powerful act of self-care and self-love, one that allows us to live more fully in the present moment and embrace the ever-changing nature of life.

As we conclude this chapter on the art of letting go, we stand poised on the brink of a new phase in our journey. Having learned to release what no longer serves us, we are now ready to turn our attention to the present moment. In the next chapter, we'll explore the practice of mindfulness and the profound benefits of living in the now. We'll discover how embracing the present moment can lead to a deeper sense of peace and fulfillment, building on the foundation of liberation we've established through the art of letting go.

"Letting go is an art that requires us to release the weight of negative thoughts and emotions. Forgiveness, both towards ourselves and others, acts as a brushstroke of liberation, painting a canvas of freedom and peace in our hearts."

4

Embracing the Present: Finding Peace in the Now

Embracing the Present: Finding Peace in the Now

As we move forward in our journey of change, we find ourselves at a critical juncture. Having delved into the depths of our past and learned the art of letting go, we now turn our attention to perhaps the most challenging aspect of personal growth: living in the present moment. This chapter explores the profound impact of mindfulness and presence on our mental well-being, offering practical strategies to cultivate a deeper connection with the here and now.

The concept of mindfulness has gained significant traction in recent years, and for good reason. At its core, mindfulness is the practice of being fully present and engaged in the current moment, without judgment or distraction. It's a deceptively simple idea that can have transformative effects on our lives. By learning to focus our attention on the present, we can reduce stress, improve our emotional regulation, and enhance our overall quality of life.

One of the primary benefits of living in the moment is the reduction of anxiety and stress. When we're caught up in thoughts about the past or worries about the future, we often miss the beauty and opportunities that exist right in front of us. By grounding ourselves in the present, we can break free from the cycle of rumination and worry that so often plagues our minds. As the renowned spiritual teacher Eckhart Tolle once said, "The present moment is all you ever have. There is never a time when your life is not 'this moment.' Is this not a fact?"

Consider for a moment how much of your day is spent thinking about things that aren't happening right now. Perhaps you're replaying a conversation from yesterday, imagining various scenarios for an upcoming meeting, or daydreaming about your next vacation. While some degree of planning and reflection is necessary, excessive mental time travel can rob us of the richness of our current experiences. By practicing mindfulness, we can learn to redirect our attention to the present moment, allowing us to fully engage with our surroundings and the people in our lives.

One of the most powerful mindfulness practices is meditation. Regular meditation has been shown to have numerous benefits for mental health, including reduced anxiety, improved emotional regulation, and increased self-awareness. To begin a meditation practice, find a quiet space where you won't be disturbed. Sit comfortably, close your eyes, and focus your attention on your breath. Notice the sensation of the air moving in and out of your body. When your mind wanders, as it inevitably will, gently bring your attention back to your breath without judgment. Start with just a few minutes a day and gradually increase the duration as you become more comfortable with the practice.

Another effective mindfulness technique is body scanning. This practice involves systematically focusing your attention on different parts of your body, from your toes to the top of your head. As you move through each area, notice any sensations you feel without trying to change them. This exercise can help you become more aware of physical sensations and tensions in your body, promoting relaxation and grounding you in the present moment.

Incorporating mindfulness into your daily routine doesn't have to be limited to formal meditation sessions. In fact, one of the most powerful ways to cultivate presence is by bringing mindful awareness to everyday activities. For example, when you're eating, take the time to fully experience your food. Notice the colors, textures, and aromas. Chew slowly and savor each bite. When you're walking, pay attention to the sensation of your feet touching the ground, the rhythm of your breath, and the sights and sounds around you. By approaching these mundane activities with curiosity and attention, we can transform them into opportunities for presence and joy.

The benefits of living in the moment extend far beyond stress reduction. When we're fully present, we're better able to connect with others, appreciate the beauty in our surroundings, and make thoughtful decisions. We become more attuned to our own needs and emotions, allowing us to respond to life's challenges with greater clarity and compassion. As Jon Kabat-Zinn, the founder of Mindfulness-Based Stress Reduction, puts it, "The little things? The little moments? They aren't little." Creating a daily routine that fosters mindfulness is crucial for reaping these benefits. Start by identifying key moments throughout your day where you can practice presence. This might include taking a few deep breaths before starting work, eating one meal mindfully each day, or taking a short mindful walk during your lunch break. The key is consistency and patience. Like any skill, mindfulness takes practice to develop. It's important to note that cultivating presence doesn't mean we never think about the past or future. Rather, it's about developing the ability to choose where we direct our attention. When we're planning for the future or reflecting on the past, we can do so intentionally and with awareness, rather than getting lost in a spiral of worry or regret. One powerful way to anchor yourself in the present is through gratitude practice. Each day, take a few moments to reflect on things you're grateful for in your current life. This could be as simple as appreciating a warm cup of coffee, the smile of a loved one, or the feeling of sunshine on your skin. By regularly acknowledging the positive aspects of our present experience, we train our minds to notice and appreciate the good in our lives, fostering a sense of contentment and presence. As we cultivate greater presence in our lives, we may encounter resistance. Our minds are often habituated to constant activity and distraction, and the practice of presence can initially feel uncomfortable or even boring. It's important to approach this process with patience and self-compassion. Remember that every moment of mindfulness, no matter how brief, is a step towards greater peace and well-being.

The journey towards living in the present moment is ongoing. There will be times when we find ourselves caught up in thoughts of the past or future, and that's okay. The key is to gently and consistently bring our attention back to the present moment, without judgment or self-criticism. As we continue this practice, we'll find that presence becomes more natural and accessible, allowing us to experience life with greater richness and clarity.

As we conclude this chapter on embracing the present, it's worth reflecting on how this practice of presence relates to our overall journey of change. By learning to fully inhabit the present moment, we create a solid foundation for personal growth and transformation. We become more aware of our thoughts, emotions, and patterns of behavior, allowing us to make conscious choices about how we want to live and who we want to become.

In the next chapter, we'll explore the healing process and the importance of nurturing our inner self. This work of inner healing is intimately connected to our ability to be present, as it requires us to face our emotions and experiences with openness and compassion. As we move forward, remember that each moment of presence is a gift - an opportunity to experience life fully and to cultivate the inner peace that is the foundation of true change.

"In the canvas of life, the present moment is the masterpiece waiting to be painted. Through mindfulness practices, we dip our brushes into the palette of now, creating strokes of tranquility and presence that color our lives with mental well-being and contentment."

5

The Healing Process: Nurturing Our Inner Self

The Healing Process: Nurturing Our Inner Self

As we continue our journey of change, we find ourselves at a crucial juncture where we must turn our attention inward and focus on the delicate process of healing. In the previous chapter, we explored the power of embracing the present moment and cultivating mindfulness. Now, we delve deeper into the intricate tapestry of our inner selves, examining the wounds that require mending and the steps we can take to nurture our emotional well-being.

The healing process is a deeply personal and often challenging endeavor. It requires us to confront the pain and trauma that we may have been carrying for years, sometimes even decades. This chapter will guide you through the stages of emotional healing, providing you with the tools and insights necessary to embark on this transformative journey.

To begin, let us consider the nature of emotional wounds. These injuries to our psyche can stem from a variety of sources: childhood experiences, relationships, professional setbacks, or even societal pressures. Regardless of their origin, these wounds have a profound impact on our daily lives, influencing our thoughts, behaviors, and relationships. Recognizing and acknowledging these wounds is the first step towards healing. The stages of emotional healing are not linear, nor are they universal. Each individual's journey is unique, shaped by their personal experiences and circumstances. However, there are common threads that weave through most healing processes. The first stage is often characterized by awareness. This is the moment when we become conscious of our pain and its impact on our lives. It can be a jarring experience, as we are forced to confront truths about ourselves that we may have long ignored or suppressed.

Following awareness comes acknowledgment. This stage requires courage, as we must accept the reality of our pain without judgment or denial. It's important to remember that acknowledging our wounds does not make us weak; on the contrary, it is a testament to our strength and our commitment to growth. As the renowned psychologist Carl Jung once said, "Until you make the unconscious conscious, it will direct your life and you will call it fate."

Once we have acknowledged our pain, we enter the stage of exploration. This is where we begin to delve deeper into the roots of our emotional wounds. We might ask ourselves questions like: Where did this pain originate? How has it manifested in my life? What beliefs or behaviors have I developed as a result of this wound? This stage often involves a great deal of introspection and can be facilitated by journaling, therapy, or open conversations with trusted friends or family members.

The exploration stage naturally leads to the phase of understanding. As we gain insights into the nature and origins of our pain, we begin to develop a more compassionate view of ourselves and our experiences. This understanding allows us to see our wounds not as inherent flaws, but as natural responses to difficult circumstances. It's in this stage that many people experience a profound shift in their self-perception, moving from self-blame to self-compassion.

With understanding comes the opportunity for release. This stage involves letting go of the negative emotions, beliefs, and patterns that have been associated with our wounds. It's important to note that release doesn't mean forgetting or dismissing our experiences. Rather, it's about freeing ourselves from the grip that these experiences have had on our present and future. Release can take many forms, from forgiveness work to symbolic rituals that help us externalize our intention to let go.

The final stage of healing is integration. This is where we begin to incorporate the lessons and growth from our healing journey into our daily lives. We develop new coping mechanisms, healthier relationship patterns, and a more balanced sense of self. Integration is an ongoing process, one that continues long after the acute phase of healing has passed.

Throughout these stages, self-care plays a crucial role in promoting healing and growth. Self-care is not about indulgence or selfishness; it's about honoring our needs and nurturing our well-being. This can involve physical practices like regular exercise, a balanced diet, and adequate sleep. It also encompasses emotional and mental practices such as meditation, journaling, or engaging in creative pursuits.

One powerful self-care practice that supports healing is mindfulness meditation. By cultivating present-moment awareness, we can learn to observe our thoughts and emotions without becoming overwhelmed by them. This creates space for healing and allows us to respond to our experiences with greater clarity and compassion. As Jon Kabat-Zinn, the founder of Mindfulness-Based Stress Reduction, eloquently puts it, "You can't stop the waves, but you can learn to surf."

Another essential aspect of self-care during the healing process is setting boundaries. As we work through our emotional wounds, we may find that certain relationships or situations trigger our pain or hinder our progress. Learning to establish and maintain healthy boundaries is a crucial skill that protects our well-being and supports our healing journey. This might involve limiting contact with toxic individuals, learning to say no to commitments that drain our energy, or creating space for solitude and reflection.

It's also important to recognize that healing is not a solitary journey. While much of the work is internal, seeking support from others can greatly enhance our healing process. This support can come in many forms: professional therapy, support groups, trusted friends, or spiritual communities. The key is to find individuals or groups that provide a safe, non-judgmental space for you to express yourself and work through your healing process.

Professional therapy, in particular, can be an invaluable resource during the healing journey. A skilled therapist can provide guidance, offer new perspectives, and teach coping strategies tailored to your specific needs. There are many different therapeutic approaches, from cognitive-behavioral therapy to psychodynamic therapy to EMDR (Eye Movement Desensitization and Reprocessing). The most important factor is finding a therapist with whom you feel comfortable and who understands your unique situation.

Support groups can also play a significant role in the healing process. Connecting with others who have experienced similar challenges can provide a sense of validation and belonging. It can be deeply comforting to know that you're not alone in your struggles. Moreover, support groups often offer practical advice and coping strategies that have worked for others, providing a wealth of resources for your own healing journey.

As we engage in these healing practices, it's crucial to approach the process with patience and self-compassion. Healing is not a linear journey, and there will likely be setbacks along the way. There may be days when old pain resurfaces, or when we fall back into familiar patterns. It's important to remember that these moments are not failures, but opportunities for deeper healing and growth.

In her book "Rising Strong," researcher and author Brené Brown writes, "The middle is messy, but it's also where the magic happens." This sentiment perfectly encapsulates the healing process. The journey through our emotional wounds can be challenging and at times overwhelming, but it's also where we discover our resilience, our strength, and our capacity for growth.

As we nurture our inner selves and progress through the stages of healing, we begin to notice subtle shifts in our daily lives. We may find ourselves responding to stressful situations with greater calm, or approaching relationships with more openness and authenticity. We might dis-

cover newfound confidence in our abilities, or a deeper sense of connection to ourselves and others. These changes, however small they may seem at first, are powerful indicators of our healing and growth.
It's also worth noting that the healing process often extends beyond our individual selves. As we heal our own wounds, we become better equipped to support others in their healing journeys. Our increased empathy and understanding can positively impact our relationships, our communities, and even society at large. In this way, personal healing becomes a catalyst for broader positive change.
As we conclude this chapter on the healing process, it's important to recognize that healing is not a destination, but an ongoing journey. Just as our lives continue to evolve and change, so too does our relationship with our emotional well-being. The skills and insights we gain through the healing process become valuable tools that we can return to again and again throughout our lives.
In the next chapter, we will explore the transformative power of acceptance. We'll examine how embracing reality, even when it's challenging, can lead to profound personal growth and positive change. This concept of acceptance builds naturally upon the healing work we've discussed here, as it requires us to approach ourselves and
our experiences with openness and compassion. As we move forward, remember that each step you take in your healing journey is a powerful act of self-love and a testament to your resilience.

"Healing is a journey of self-nurturing, a process that requires us to tend to our emotional wounds with care and compassion. By practicing self-care and seeking support from others, we water the seeds of healing within us, allowing growth and transformation to blossom."

6

Acceptance: The Key to Transformation

RAJENDRA SINGH VAGHELA

Acceptance: The Key to Transformation

As we journey through the process of letting go and embracing change, we arrive at a crucial waypoint: acceptance. This chapter builds upon the healing process we explored previously, guiding us towards a transformative understanding of acceptance and its pivotal role in personal growth. Acceptance is not merely a passive state of resignation, but rather an active embrace of reality that opens the door to profound personal transformation.

Acceptance, in its truest form, is the acknowledgment and embrace of what is, without resistance or denial. It is the recognition that our reality, whether pleasant or challenging, is the foundation from which all change must spring. This concept may seem counterintuitive at first glance. After all, isn't change about altering our circumstances rather than accepting them? The paradox lies in the fact that genuine, lasting change can only occur when we first accept our current state of being. Consider the words of Carl Jung, the renowned psychiatrist and psychoanalyst, who said, "We cannot change anything until we accept it. Condemnation does not liberate, it oppresses." This profound statement encapsulates the essence of acceptance as a catalyst for transformation.

When we resist or condemn our current circumstances, we expend enormous amounts of energy fighting against reality. This struggle not only depletes us but also keeps us anchored to the very situations we wish to change.

The practice of acceptance does not mean we approve of or enjoy every aspect of our lives. Rather, it means we recognize and acknowledge our current reality without judgment. This non-judgmental stance creates space for clarity and insight, allowing us to see our situations more objectively and identify potential paths forward.

One of the most powerful techniques for cultivating acceptance is mindfulness meditation. This practice involves observing our thoughts, feelings, and sensations without attempting to change or judge them. By regularly engaging in mindfulness, we train ourselves to accept the present moment as it is, rather than as we wish it to be. This skill translates into our daily lives, helping us navigate challenging situations with greater equanimity.

Another effective strategy for fostering acceptance is the practice of cognitive reframing. This technique involves consciously shifting our perspective on a situation to view it in a more balanced or positive light. For example, instead of viewing a job loss as a catastrophic failure, we might reframe it as an opportunity for career exploration and growth. This shift in perspective doesn't change the fact of the job loss, but it does change our relationship to it, opening up new possibilities for action and growth.

Acceptance also plays a crucial role in our relationships with others. When we practice acceptance in our interpersonal interactions, we create space for authenticity and deeper connection. This doesn't mean we tolerate harmful behavior, but rather that we accept people for who they are, recognizing that we cannot change others, only ourselves.

The renowned spiritual teacher Eckhart Tolle emphasizes this point, stating, "Accept - then act. Whatever the present moment contains, accept it as if you had chosen it. Always work with it, not against it." This approach to life's challenges can be transformative, allowing us to channel our energy into constructive action rather than futile resistance.

Real-life examples abound of how acceptance leads to positive change. Consider the story of Nick Vujicic, born without limbs. Instead of succumbing to despair or bitterness, Nick accepted his physical condition and chose to focus on what he could do rather than what he couldn't. This acceptance became the foundation for an extraordinary life as a motivational speaker, author, and advocate for people with disabilities.

Another powerful example is that of Nelson Mandela. During his 27 years of imprisonment, Mandela came to accept his circumstances, using his time to deepen his understanding of himself and his oppressors. This acceptance did not diminish his commitment to change but rather strengthened his resolve and allowed him to emerge as a unifying leader capable of guiding South Africa through a peaceful transition from apartheid.

These stories illustrate that acceptance is not about passive resignation but about aligning ourselves with reality in a way that empowers us to effect meaningful change. When we accept our circumstances, we free up the mental and emotional resources previously spent on resistance, allowing us to channel that energy into growth and transformation. Cultivating acceptance in difficult situations requires practice and patience. One effective technique is the use of acceptance statements. These are simple phrases we can repeat to ourselves when facing challenging circumstances. For example, "This is happening, and I can handle it," or "I accept this moment as it is." These statements help to shift our mindset from resistance to acceptance, even in the face of adversity. Another powerful tool for fostering acceptance is gratitude practice. By regularly acknowledging and appreciating the positive aspects of our lives, we cultivate a mindset of acceptance that extends to all areas of our experience. This doesn't mean ignoring or minimizing difficulties, but rather developing a more balanced perspective that recognizes both challenges and blessings.

It's important to note that acceptance doesn't mean we become complacent or stop striving for positive change. On the contrary, true acceptance provides the stable foundation from which meaningful change can occur. When we accept our current reality, we see it clearly, without the distortions of denial or wishful thinking. This clarity allows us to make informed decisions about how to move forward.

The transformative power of acceptance extends beyond our individual lives to our collective experience as well. In a world often characterized by conflict and division, the practice of acceptance can be a powerful force for healing and unity. When we learn to accept differences in others, we open the door to dialogue, understanding, and collaboration. As we conclude this exploration of acceptance, it's clear that this principle is indeed a key to transformation. By embracing what is, we paradoxically create the conditions for change. We free ourselves from the exhausting struggle against reality and open ourselves to new possibilities. As we move forward in our journey of change, let us carry with us this understanding of acceptance as a powerful tool for personal growth and transformation.

In the next chapter, we will delve into the concept of a growth mindset and explore how our perspectives shape our ability to embrace change. This shift in how we view challenges and opportunities will build upon the foundation of acceptance we've established, further empowering us to navigate the journey of change with resilience and optimism.

"Acceptance is the key that unlocks the door to personal transformation. By embracing acceptance in the face of adversity, we pave the path to growth and resilience. Like a sculptor shaping a masterpiece, we mold our lives with acceptance, creating beauty out of challenges."

7
Growth Mindset: Shifting Perspectives

Growth Mindset: Shifting Perspectives

As we journey through the process of letting go and embracing change, we arrive at a crucial juncture where our perspective on growth and learning plays a pivotal role. Building upon the foundation of acceptance we explored in the previous chapter, we now turn our attention to the power of cultivating a growth mindset. This shift in perspective can dramatically alter how we approach challenges, setbacks, and opportunities for personal development.

The concept of a growth mindset, first introduced by psychologist Carol Dweck, stands in stark contrast to what is known as a fixed mindset. At its core, a growth mindset is the belief that our abilities and intelligence can be developed through dedication, hard work, and a willingness to learn from our experiences. This perspective views challenges as opportunities for growth rather than threats to our self-image. On the other hand, a fixed mindset assumes that our qualities are static and unchangeable, leading to a tendency to avoid challenges and give up easily in the face of obstacles.

To truly understand the impact of these mindsets, let's delve deeper into their characteristics and consequences. Those with a fixed mindset often believe that talent alone creates success, without the need for effort. They may feel threatened by the success of others, viewing it as a reflection of their own inadequacies. This mindset can lead to a constant need to prove oneself and a fear of failure that ultimately limits personal growth and achievement. Dweck notes, "The passion for stretching yourself and sticking to it, even (or especially) when it's not going well, is the hallmark of the growth mindset. This is the mindset that allows people to thrive during some of the most challenging times in their lives."

In contrast, individuals with a growth mindset embrace challenges as opportunities to learn and improve. They persist in the face of setbacks, seeing effort as the path to mastery. Criticism is viewed as valuable feedback rather than a personal attack, and the success of others becomes a source of inspiration and learning. This mindset fosters a love for learning and a resilience that is essential for great accomplishment in any field.

The implications of adopting a growth mindset extend far beyond academic or professional settings. It influences our relationships, our ability to cope with change, and our overall sense of fulfillment in life. When we believe in our capacity to grow and change, we become more open to new experiences and more willing to take risks that can lead to personal and professional advancement.

However, it's important to recognize that shifting from a fixed to a growth mindset is not an overnight process. It requires consistent effort and a willingness to challenge our ingrained beliefs about ourselves and our abilities. One powerful strategy for developing a growth mindset is to pay attention to our self-talk. When faced with a challenge, notice the internal dialogue that arises. Are you telling yourself that you're not good enough or that you'll never be able to succeed? This is the voice of the fixed mindset. Challenge these thoughts by reframing them in terms of growth and learning. Instead of "I can't do this," try "I can't do this yet, but I can learn with practice."

Another effective technique is to embrace the power of "yet." This simple word can transform our perception of our abilities and potential. When we say, "I'm not good at public speaking," we're reinforcing a fixed mindset. But when we add "yet" to the end of that statement – "I'm not good at public speaking yet" – we open up the possibility for improvement and growth. This subtle shift in language can have a profound impact on our motivation and perseverance.

Cultivating curiosity is another cornerstone of developing a growth mindset. When we approach new situations with genuine curiosity rather than judgment or fear, we create opportunities for learning and growth. Ask questions, seek out new experiences, and be willing to step outside your comfort zone. Each new experience, whether successful or not, becomes a chance to learn and develop.

In our daily lives, we can practice adopting a growth mindset by setting learning goals rather than performance goals. Instead of focusing solely on achieving a specific outcome, shift your attention to what you can learn from the process. For example, rather than aiming to get a promotion at work, set a goal to develop new skills that will make you a stronger candidate for future opportunities. This approach not only increases your chances of success but also ensures that you're growing and learning regardless of the immediate outcome.

It's also crucial to recognize and celebrate effort, not just results. In a growth mindset, the process of learning and improving is valued as much as, if not more than, the final achievement. Take time to acknowledge the hard work you've put into a project, even if the end result isn't exactly what you hoped for. This practice helps to reinforce the idea that effort and persistence are key to growth and success.

Embracing failure as a learning opportunity is perhaps one of the most challenging aspects of developing a growth mindset. In a fixed mindset, failure is seen as a definitive statement about one's abilities. In a growth mindset, failure is viewed as a temporary setback and a valuable source of information. When you encounter a setback, take time to reflect on what you can learn from the experience. What would you do differently next time? What new skills or knowledge do you need to acquire to improve your chances of success?

The impact of adopting a growth mindset extends beyond individual growth; it can transform entire organizations and communities. Leaders who foster a growth mindset in their teams create environments where innovation thrives, employees feel valued for their efforts and contributions, and continuous learning is the norm. In education, teachers who promote a growth mindset in their students can dramatically improve academic performance and student engagement.

As we cultivate a growth mindset, we begin to see challenges as opportunities rather than threats. We become more resilient in the face of setbacks and more open to feedback and constructive criticism. This shift in perspective allows us to approach change with curiosity and optimism rather than fear and resistance. It empowers us to take control of our personal growth and to view our potential as limitless.

In the context of our journey of letting go and embracing change, a growth mindset becomes a powerful tool for transformation. It allows us to release our attachment to fixed ideas about who we are and what we're capable of. Instead, we open ourselves up to the possibility of continuous growth and improvement. This mindset enables us to approach the process of change with courage and enthusiasm, knowing that each challenge we face is an opportunity to learn and evolve.

As we move forward in our exploration of change and personal growth, we'll build upon this foundation of a growth mindset to discover the joy that can be found in transition and transformation. The next chapter will delve into the beauty of change, exploring how we can not only accept but celebrate the transitions in our lives. We'll examine stories of individuals who have found profound joy and fulfillment through embracing change, and we'll explore activities that can help us recognize and appreciate our own growth journey. By combining the power of a growth mindset with an appreciation for the beauty of change, we set the stage for a life of continuous learning, growth, and fulfillment.

"In the garden of the mind, a growth mindset blooms like a resilient flower, while a fixed mindset remains stagnant like unwatered soil. Embracing growth mindset opens the door to endless possibilities and learning, nurturing a mindset that thrives on challenges and sees failures as stepping stones to success."

8
The Beauty of Change: Finding Joy in Transition

RAJENDRA SINGH VAGHELA

The Beauty of Change: Finding Joy in Transition

As we progress through our journey of change, we arrive at a pivotal moment where we can begin to appreciate the beauty inherent in the process of transformation. This chapter marks a significant shift in perspective, moving from the challenges and difficulties of change to the joy and wonder it can bring into our lives. Building upon the growth mindset we cultivated in the previous chapter, we now turn our attention to celebrating the positive aspects of change and finding genuine happiness in the midst of transition.

Change, by its very nature, can be disruptive and unsettling. It often pushes us out of our comfort zones and challenges our established routines and beliefs. However, it is precisely this disruption that creates the space for new experiences, personal growth, and unexpected joys. As the renowned author C.S. Lewis once said, "It may be hard for an egg to turn into a bird: it would be a jolly sight harder for it to learn to fly while remaining an egg. We are like eggs at present. And you cannot go on indefinitely being just an ordinary, decent egg. We must be hatched or go bad." This poignant metaphor beautifully illustrates the necessity and beauty of change in our lives.

One of the most profound ways to find joy in transition is to recognize and appreciate the personal growth that occurs during times of change. Every challenge we face, every obstacle we overcome, contributes to our development as individuals. These experiences shape our character, strengthen our resilience, and expand our understanding of ourselves and the world around us. By consciously acknowledging these positive outcomes, we can begin to view change not as a source of stress or anxiety, but as an opportunity for growth and self-discovery.

Consider the story of Sarah, a marketing executive who found herself unexpectedly laid off from her high-powered corporate job. Initially, Sarah was devastated by this sudden change in her career trajectory. She had defined herself by her professional success for so long that she felt lost without her prestigious title and corner office. However, as she navigated this period of transition, Sarah began to discover aspects of herself that had long been neglected in pursuit of her career goals.

With newfound free time, Sarah rediscovered her passion for painting, a hobby she had abandoned years ago due to the demands of her job. As she immersed herself in her art, she found a sense of fulfillment and joy that had been missing from her life for years. The change that initially seemed like a catastrophe became the catalyst for a profound personal transformation. Sarah's story illustrates how even seemingly negative changes can lead to unexpected sources of happiness and self-discovery.

Another key aspect of finding joy in transition is learning to embrace uncertainty. Often, our fear of the unknown prevents us from fully engaging with the present moment and appreciating the opportunities that change brings. By cultivating a sense of curiosity and openness to new experiences, we can transform our relationship with uncertainty. Instead of viewing it as a threat, we can see it as an exciting adventure, full of potential and possibility.

The renowned spiritual teacher Eckhart Tolle speaks to this idea when he says, "Some changes look negative on the surface but you will soon realize that space is being created in your life for something new to emerge." This perspective invites us to trust in the process of change, even when we cannot see the ultimate outcome. By maintaining an attitude of openness and curiosity, we allow ourselves to be surprised and delighted by the unexpected gifts that change can bring.

One powerful way to cultivate joy in transition is to practice gratitude. When we're in the midst of change, it's easy to focus on what we've lost or what's difficult about our current situation. However, by intentionally directing our attention to the things we're grateful for, we can shift our emotional state and find moments of joy even in challenging circumstances. This doesn't mean ignoring or suppressing difficult emotions, but rather creating a balance by also acknowledging the positive aspects of our experience.

Consider keeping a gratitude journal during times of transition. Each day, write down three things you're grateful for, no matter how small they may seem. This practice can help train your mind to notice and appreciate the positive aspects of your life, even as you navigate change. Over time, you may find that this habit not only increases your sense of joy and well-being but also helps you maintain a more balanced perspective on the changes you're experiencing.

Another powerful tool for finding joy in transition is to connect with others who are going through similar experiences. Sharing our stories, challenges, and triumphs with others can provide a sense of community and support that is invaluable during times of change. These connections can also offer new perspectives and insights that we might not have discovered on our own.

Consider the story of Mark, who found himself struggling to adjust after moving to a new city for work. Feeling isolated and overwhelmed, Mark decided to join a local meetup group for newcomers to the area. Through this group, he not only made new friends but also discovered hidden gems in his new city that he might never have found on his own. The joy he found in these new connections and experiences transformed his perception of the move from a stressful upheaval to an exciting new chapter in his life.

As we learn to find joy in transition, it's important to remember that this is a skill that can be developed over time. Like any skill, it requires practice and patience. There may be days when joy feels elusive, and that's okay. The key is to maintain a compassionate attitude towards ourselves and to trust in the process of change.

One effective way to cultivate this skill is through mindfulness practices. By learning to be fully present in the moment, we can more easily recognize and appreciate the small joys that exist even in the midst of significant change. This might involve taking a few minutes each day to practice mindful breathing, or simply pausing throughout the day to fully engage with your current experience, whether it's savoring a cup of coffee or noticing the beauty of a sunset.

As we conclude this chapter, it's important to recognize that finding joy in transition is not about denying the challenges or difficulties that come with change. Rather, it's about expanding our perspective to include the potential for growth, discovery, and happiness that exists within these experiences. By cultivating gratitude, embracing uncertainty, connecting with others, and practicing mindfulness, we can learn to navigate change with greater ease and find genuine joy in the process of transformation.

As we move forward, we'll explore another crucial aspect of navigating change: building resilience. This skill will complement our ability to find joy in transition, providing us with the strength and flexibility needed to face life's challenges with grace and courage. The journey of change is ongoing, and as we continue to develop these skills, we'll find ourselves better equipped to embrace the ever-evolving nature of life, finding beauty and meaning in each new phase of our personal growth.

"Change, like a butterfly emerging from its cocoon, brings forth beauty and transformation. Through stories of individuals who danced with change and found joy in transition, we learn to appreciate the colors of transformation and celebrate the journey of growth. By engaging in activities that recognize personal growth, we paint our lives with the hues of resilience and joy."

9

Building Resilience: Strength in the Face of Adversity

Building Resilience: Strength in the Face of Adversity

As we move from the joy and celebration of positive change explored in the previous chapter, we now turn our attention to a crucial aspect of navigating life's challenges: resilience. Building resilience is not just about weathering storms; it's about learning to dance in the rain and finding strength in the face of adversity.

Defining resilience and its importance in navigating change Resilience is often described as the ability to bounce back from adversity, but it's much more than that. It's the capacity to adapt, grow, and even thrive in the face of challenges, stress, and trauma. Psychologist Ann Masten refers to resilience as "ordinary magic," highlighting that it's not a rare quality possessed by a few extraordinary individuals, but rather a common capacity that can be cultivated and strengthened in everyone.

In the context of change, resilience is particularly crucial. Change, whether chosen or thrust upon us, often brings uncertainty and discomfort. It can shake the foundations of our identity and challenge our sense of security. Resilient individuals are better equipped to navigate these turbulent waters, maintaining their course even when faced with unexpected obstacles.

Dr. George Bonanno, a professor of clinical psychology at Columbia University, has spent decades studying resilience. His research suggests that resilience is far more common than we might think. In his book "The Other Side of Sadness," he writes, "The most common response to potential trauma is resilience... The majority of people who experience a potentially traumatic event do not develop PTSD or any other disorder." This insight is both comforting and empowering, reminding us that we are inherently capable of overcoming adversity.

However, recognizing our innate capacity for resilience doesn't mean we should take it for granted. Like any skill, resilience can be honed and strengthened through intentional practice and the development of specific strategies. As we face increasingly complex and rapidly changing environments in our personal and professional lives, cultivating resilience becomes not just beneficial, but essential.

Techniques for building resilience in everyday life

Building resilience isn't about grand gestures or heroic acts. Instead, it's about small, consistent actions and mindset shifts that, over time, create a robust foundation for facing life's challenges. Here are several techniques that can help foster resilience in your daily life:

Cultivate a growth mindset: As we explored in Chapter 7, adopting a growth mindset can significantly impact our ability to navigate change. When facing challenges, view them as opportunities for learning and growth rather than insurmountable obstacles. This perspective shift can transform setbacks into stepping stones.

Practice self-compassion: Be kind to yourself, especially during difficult times. Dr. Kristin Neff, a pioneer in self-compassion research, argues that self-compassion is more beneficial than self-esteem in building resilience. In her words, "With self-compassion, we give ourselves the same kindness and care we'd give to a good friend." This approach allows us to acknowledge our struggles without harsh self-judgment, fostering emotional resilience.

Develop problem-solving skills: Enhance your ability to break down complex problems into manageable parts. When faced with a challenge, take a step back, analyze the situation, and consider multiple approaches. This analytical skill not only helps in finding solutions but also instills a sense of control and agency in difficult situations.

Maintain perspective: Remember that most challenges are temporary. Cultivate the ability to see the bigger picture, even in the midst of a crisis. This doesn't mean minimizing your current struggles, but rather recognizing that they are part of a larger life journey.

Build a strong support network: Surround yourself with supportive, positive people. Having a reliable support system can provide emotional comfort, practical assistance, and different perspectives when you're facing challenges. As the saying goes, "A problem shared is a problem halved."

Practice mindfulness: Regular mindfulness practice can enhance your ability to stay present and manage stress effectively. Mindfulness helps in recognizing and accepting emotions without being overwhelmed by them, a crucial skill in building emotional resilience.

Set and pursue meaningful goals: Having a sense of purpose can anchor you during turbulent times. Set both short-term and long-term goals that align with your values and work steadily towards them. This provides a sense of direction and accomplishment, bolstering your resilience.

Take care of your physical health: The mind-body connection is powerful. Regular exercise, adequate sleep, and a balanced diet can significantly enhance your ability to cope with stress and bounce back from adversity.

Learn from past experiences: Reflect on how you've overcome challenges in the past. What strategies worked? What strengths did you draw upon? Use these insights to build confidence in your ability to handle future challenges.

Embrace change: As we've explored throughout this book, change is an inevitable part of life. Rather than resisting it, practice embracing change as an opportunity for growth and new experiences. This mindset shift can transform potential threats into exciting challenges.

The role of community and support systems in fostering resilience

While personal strategies are crucial in building resilience, the importance of community and support systems cannot be overstated. Humans are inherently social creatures, and our connections with others play a vital role in our ability to navigate life's challenges.

Research consistently shows that individuals with strong social support networks are more resilient in the face of adversity. This support can come from various sources: family, friends, colleagues, mentors, or even community groups. These connections provide not just emotional comfort, but also practical assistance, diverse perspectives, and a sense of belonging that can be crucial during difficult times.

Dr. Emmy Werner, a developmental psychologist known for her groundbreaking study on resilience in children, found that the most resilient individuals had at least one person in their lives who unconditionally accepted them. This highlights the powerful impact that even a single supportive relationship can have on our ability to overcome challenges.

Community support goes beyond individual relationships. Being part of a community – whether it's a neighborhood, a religious group, a hobby club, or a professional network – can provide a sense of identity and purpose that bolsters resilience. Communities often rally around members in times of need, offering both tangible and intangible support.

Moreover, communities can serve as platforms for shared experiences and collective wisdom. Hearing stories of how others have overcome similar challenges can inspire hope and provide practical strategies. Support groups, for instance, can be powerful tools for building resilience, allowing individuals to share their struggles, learn from others, and realize they're not alone in their experiences.

In the workplace, fostering a supportive environment can significantly enhance collective resilience. Organizations that prioritize open communication, teamwork, and employee well-being often find their teams more adaptable and resilient in the face of challenges. As management expert Peter Senge notes, "Organizations learn only through individuals who learn. Individual learning does not guarantee organizational learning. But without it, no organizational learning occurs."

It's important to note that building and maintaining support systems requires effort and intention. It involves being willing to reach out, to be vulnerable, and to offer support to others in return. In our increasingly digital world, it's easy to feel connected yet isolated. Making an effort to cultivate deep, meaningful relationships and actively engage with our communities can significantly enhance our resilience.

As we conclude this chapter on resilience, it's clear that this quality is not just about individual strength, but about our connections to others and our ability to draw upon both internal and external resources. Resilience is a dynamic process, one that we can continually develop and strengthen throughout our lives.

In the face of change and adversity, resilience allows us not just to survive, but to thrive. It enables us to maintain hope, to find meaning in our struggles, and to emerge from challenges stronger and wiser. As we move into our final chapter, we'll

explore how all the concepts we've discussed – from acknowledging our past to embracing change and building resilience – come together to pave the way for new beginnings. We'll see how the journey of letting go ultimately leads us to a place of renewed possibility and potential.

"Resilience is the armor that shields us in the battlefield of change, fortifying our spirits against adversity. By defining resilience as the art of bouncing back from challenges, we equip ourselves with techniques to build resilience in our daily lives. Just as a tree stands tall with deep roots, our community and support systems nourish our resilience, helping us weather the storms of change."

10
A New Moon : Embracing New Beginnings

A New Moon : Embracing New Beginnings

As we reach the final chapter of our journey through change, we find ourselves at a new moon - a symbol of fresh beginnings and untapped potential. Much like the moon's cycle, we have traversed through various phases of transformation, and now stand at the threshold of a new cycle. This chapter, aptly titled "A New Moon: Embracing New Beginnings," serves as both a culmination of our exploration and a launching pad for the next phase of your personal growth.

The significance of new beginnings cannot be overstated in the context of personal transformation. Throughout history, cultures around the world have recognized the power of fresh starts. The ancient Romans dedicated the first month of their calendar, January, to Janus, the god of beginnings and transitions. In many Eastern philosophies, the concept of rebirth or reincarnation underscores the cyclical nature of existence and the opportunity for renewal. Even in modern psychology, the idea of a "clean slate" or a "fresh start" is often used as a powerful motivational tool.

New beginnings offer us a psychological reset, a chance to leave behind old habits, outdated beliefs, and past mistakes. They provide a sense of hope and possibility that can be incredibly empowering. As the renowned author Melody Beattie once said, "The new year stands before us, like a chapter in a book, waiting to be written. We can help write that story by setting goals." This sentiment applies not just to new years, but to any moment we choose to embrace as a new beginning.

However, it's important to recognize that new beginnings don't always align with external markers like calendar dates or life events. True new beginnings often start internally, with a shift in perspective or a decision to change. They can happen at any moment, sparked by a sudden realization, a gradual awakening, or a conscious choice to move in a new direction. The key is to remain open to these opportunities for renewal and to actively cultivate them in our lives.

One powerful way to embrace new beginnings is through the practice of setting intentions. Unlike traditional goal-setting, which often focuses on specific outcomes, setting intentions is about aligning our actions with our values and desired way of being. It's less about achieving particular results and more about living in a way that reflects our true selves and aspirations.

To set meaningful intentions, start by reflecting on what truly matters to you. What values do you want to embody more fully? What qualities do you want to cultivate in yourself? Perhaps you want to be more compassionate, more courageous, or more creative. Maybe you aspire to live with greater purpose or to contribute more to your community. Whatever your intentions, make sure they resonate deeply with your authentic self.

Once you've identified your intentions, consider how you can integrate them into your daily life. This might involve creating new habits, adjusting your routines, or simply bringing more mindfulness to your actions. For example, if your intention is to be more compassionate, you might practice random acts of kindness or set aside time each day for loving-kindness meditation. If you intend to live with greater purpose, you might start each morning by reflecting on how you can align your day's activities with your core values.

Remember, the power of intentions lies not in their perfection, but in their practice. As the spiritual teacher Deepak Chopra notes, "Intention is much more powerful when it comes from a place of contentment than if it arises from a sense of lack or need. Stay centered and refuse to be influenced by other people's doubts or criticisms." Be patient with yourself as you work to embody your intentions, and celebrate the small victories along the way.

While setting intentions provides direction for your new beginning, personal goals can offer concrete steps toward manifesting those intentions. Goals give shape to our aspirations and provide measurable markers of progress. However, it's crucial to approach goal-setting with mindfulness and flexibility.

When setting personal goals, consider using the SMART framework: Specific, Measurable, Achievable, Relevant, and Time-bound. This approach helps ensure that your goals are clear and attainable. For instance, instead of a vague goal like "become healthier," you might set a SMART goal such as "practice yoga for 30 minutes, three times a week, for the next three months."

At the same time, remember that goals are meant to serve you, not constrain you. Be willing to adjust your goals as you grow and change. Sometimes, the process of working towards a goal teaches us that what we truly want is different from what we initially thought. Embrace this as part of your journey of self-discovery.

It's also important to balance ambitious long-term goals with smaller, more immediately achievable ones. Small wins can provide the motivation and confidence needed to tackle bigger challenges. As the saying goes, "How do you eat an elephant? One bite at a time." Break down your larger goals into manageable steps, and celebrate each milestone along the way.

As you embark on this new phase of your journey, remember that change is not a destination but an ongoing process. The work you've done throughout this book - acknowledging your shadows, letting go of what no longer serves you, embracing the present, nurturing your inner self, cultivating acceptance, developing a growth mindset, finding joy in transition, and building resilience - these are all practices that you can continue to refine and deepen.

The journey of change doesn't end with the closing of this book. In fact, in many ways, it's just beginning. As you move forward, you may find yourself cycling through these phases again and again, each time with new insights and deeper understanding. This is not a sign of failure or lack of progress; rather, it's a testament to the spiral nature of growth and transformation.

Remember the metaphor of the moon's phases that we started with. Just as the moon continually cycles through its phases, so too will you experience cycles of growth, change, and renewal. There will be times of darkness, when change feels challenging or even impossible. But just as the new moon always follows the dark moon, new beginnings are always possible.

As you continue on your path, stay connected to your inner wisdom. Trust the insights you've gained and the strengths you've developed. At the same time, remain open to new learning and new perspectives. Seek out sources of inspiration and support that resonate with you, whether that's through books, mentors, community groups, or spiritual practices. Above all, be kind to yourself. Change is not always easy, and there will likely be setbacks and struggles along the way. Treat these as opportunities for learning and growth rather than as failures. As the Buddhist teacher Pema Chödrön wisely advises, "To be fully alive, fully human, and completely awake is to be continually thrown out of the nest. To live fully is to be always in no-man's-land, to experience each moment as completely new and fresh."

As we conclude this chapter and this book, let's return to the image of the new moon. In its darkness lies infinite potential - just as in you lies the potential for continual growth and transformation. Each new moon, each new beginning, offers a chance to realign with your truest self, to let go of what no longer serves you, and to step more fully into the life you envision.

May you embrace each new beginning with courage, curiosity, and compassion. May you find joy in the journey of change, knowing that with each step, you are becoming more fully yourself. And may you always remember that, like the moon, you have the inherent ability to renew yourself, to shine brightly, and to inspire others with your light.

"Like the new moon that heralds fresh beginnings, we stand at the threshold of a new chapter in our lives. Setting intentions for the future and personal goals becomes the compass that guides us towards our dreams. As the book closes, it whispers words of encouragement, reminding us that the journey of change continues beyond these pages, inviting us to embrace new beginnings with open hearts and minds."

Conclusion

Throughout "Letting Go: A Journey of Change," we've explored the transformative power of embracing life's natural cycles. Like the moon's phases, our lives are in constant flux, presenting opportunities for growth and renewal. We've learned that acknowledging our past, including its shadows, is crucial for moving forward.

The art of letting go emerged as a central theme, offering strategies to release what no longer serves us. We discovered the importance of living in the present moment and nurturing our inner selves through mindfulness and self-care practices. Acceptance was revealed as a key to personal transformation, allowing us to navigate life's challenges with greater ease.

We explored the power of a growth mindset in reshaping our perspectives and embracing change. The beauty of transformation was highlighted through inspiring stories and practical exercises, encouraging readers to find joy in their own journeys. Building resilience emerged as a vital skill for facing adversity and continuing our path of personal growth.

As we conclude this journey, remember that change is not just inevitable, but also an opportunity for renewal and growth. Like the new moon, each of us has the potential for fresh starts and new beginnings. The tools and insights shared in this book are not just concepts, but invitations to continue your personal journey of change long after you've turned the final page.

May you approach each phase of your life with curiosity, compassion, and courage. Embrace the ebb and flow of your experiences, knowing that each moment offers a chance to let go of what no longer serves you and welcome new possibilities. Your journey of change is uniquely yours – honor it, nurture it, and allow it to unfold with grace and purpose.

Sajjna doori enni v na rakhi
Tu kol aawe
Te menu chah na howey
Written by - Jayprakash bishnoi